Session Skills
for Keyboards
Initial-Grade 2

Published by
Trinity College London
www.trinitycollege.com

Registered in England
Company no. 02683033
Charity no. 1014792

Printed in England by Caligraving Ltd.
Written, recorded and produced by Camden Music Services.
Exercises devised by Jane Watkins, backing tracks by Tom Fleming.

SESSION SKILLS   CONTENTS

SESSION SKILLS

INTRODUCTION

To be a great rock and pop musician you need to develop a range of important musical skills – from performing with flair to improvising and picking up new songs quickly. Trinity College London's Rock & Pop exams are designed to help you develop these skills and take your musicianship to the next level.

An important part of each Rock & Pop exam is the **session skills** test. For this you can choose either **playback** or **improvising**:

- ⚡ **Playback** involves playing some music you have not seen or heard before, testing your ability to pick up new musical material quickly

- ⚡ **Improvising** involves performing an improvisation over a backing track, testing your ability to respond creatively to a specified musical style and chord sequence.

About this book

This book is specially designed to help you prepare for the session skills test at Initial to Grade 2, whether you choose playback or improvising. It contains plenty of example tests to use for practice, as well as a CD of backing tracks. It also includes specific guidance on how to approach playback and improvising at Initial, Grade 1 and Grade 2.

Please note that Rock & Pop exams require you to perform three songs as well as the session skills test. A range of songs for each grade level are provided in a separate series of Rock & Pop song books, also published by Trinity. Additional songs can be downloaded at www.trinityrock.com, where you can also find the syllabus and a range of resources for teaching and learning. The syllabus can change from time to time, so check the website regularly to make sure you are referring to an up-to-date version.

SESSION SKILLS

THE TESTS

Playback

If you choose playback for the session skills test, you'll be asked to perform some music you have not seen or heard before. You'll be given a song chart and 30 seconds to study it and try out any sections. The examiner will then play the backing track.

You should listen to the backing track, playing back what you hear and reading the music from the song chart if you want. You'll hear a series of short melodic phrases – you should repeat each of these straight back in turn. A count-in will be given at the beginning of the backing track, and a backing rhythm will play throughout.

In the exam you'll have two chances to play along with the backing track: first time for practice and second time for assessment. If you choose to read the music from the song chart, remember that for each repeated phrase you should listen the first time and play the second time.

Improvising

If you choose improvising for the session skills test, you'll be asked to improvise in a specific style over a backing track you have not heard before. You'll be given a chord chart, and the examiner will play a short section of the backing track to give you a feel for the tempo and style. You'll have 30 seconds to study the chord chart and try out any sections. The examiner will then play the backing track.

You should improvise in the specified style over the backing track, which will consist of four repetitions of the chord sequence shown on the chord chart. A count-in will be given at the beginning of the backing track, and a backing rhythm will play throughout.

In the exam you'll have two chances to play along with the backing track: first time for practice and second time for assessment. A count-in will be given both times.

SESSION SKILLS

PARAMETERS

Trinity provides a full set of parameters for the session skills tests. Published online at www.trinityrock.com, these tell you which musical elements are featured in improvising and playback at each grade. All the example tests in this book have been written to fit with these parameters, so you can be sure that the test in the exam will be similar to the examples in this book.

The following is a summary of the parameters for Initial to Grade 2. Visit www.trinityrock.com for the full set of parameters across all grades.

Playback

For keyboard players at Initial to Grade 2, playback is always eight bars long. Within this, each phrase is two bars long, making a total of four phrases. At Initial and Grade 1 the time signature can be $\frac{2}{4}$ or $\frac{4}{4}$, and at Grade 2 it can also be $\frac{3}{4}$.

You can expect to see minims (half notes) and crotchets (quarter notes) in playback at Initial, with some crotchet rests. At Grade 1 semibreves (whole notes) and quavers (eight notes) can also appear, as well as semibreve and minim rests. At Grade 2 there can also be dotted minims and ties.

No dynamics feature at Initial, but p and f are used at Grade 1 and 2, so to try to observe these dynamics where they appear. At Grade 2 there can also be accents. At Initial the key is either C major or A minor, with G major and E minor also appearing at Grade 1, and F major and D minor appearing at Grade 2.

Playback at Initial is for the right hand only, in five-finger hand position. At Grade 1 a simple left hand part is added, only in two bars. At Grade 2 both hands play throughout, and there may be some small shifts of hand position.

Improvising

For keyboard players at Initial to Grade 2, the chord sequence is always four bars long with one chord per bar. The backing track consists of four repetitions of this sequence, requiring an improvisation that lasts 16 bars in total. The time signature is always $\frac{4}{4}$ at Initial and Grade 1. At Grade 2 it can also be $\frac{3}{4}$.

At Initial the chord sequence can be in C major or G major. At Grade 1 it can also be in A minor or C minor, and at Grade 2 it can be in F major, D major and D minor. Chords I, IV and V are mainly featured at Initial, with chords on any degree of the scale (simple major and minor chords only) introduced at Grade 1 and Grade 2. Chords are notated at Initial and Grade 1 in addition to chord symbols being provided. Chords symbols only are provided at Grade 2.

Improvising at Initial is in either simple rock or pop style. At Grade 1 it can also be in ballad or heavy rock style, with country style appearing at Grade 2.

INITIAL   PLAYBACK

Example 1

Example 2

Example 3

Example 4

TOP TIP Remember that to perform the playback test you can read from the song chart or copy what you hear by listening to the backing track – or both. It's up to you and there is no right or wrong way of doing it.

Example 5

Example 6

Example 7

Example 8

Example 9

Example 10

INITIAL IMPROVISING

Example 1

♩ = 90 **Simple Rock**

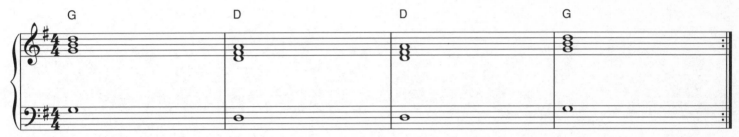

Example 2

♩ = 80 **Pop**

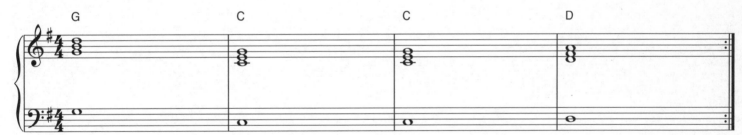

Example 3

♩ = 100 **Simple Rock**

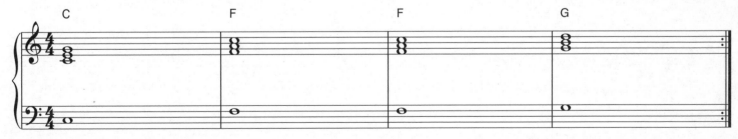

Example 4

$\flat$ = 90 **Simple Rock**

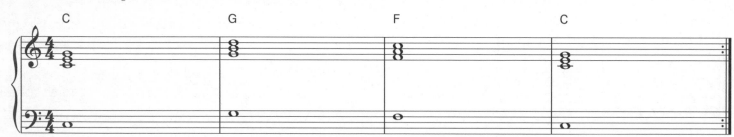

TOP TIP You don't have to fill your whole improvisation with notes - remember that you can also use rests, or silences. Can you practise using rests in your improvisations to make some effective contrasts with the notes?

Example 5

$\flat$ = 90 **Pop**

Example 6

$\flat$ = 120 **Simple Rock**

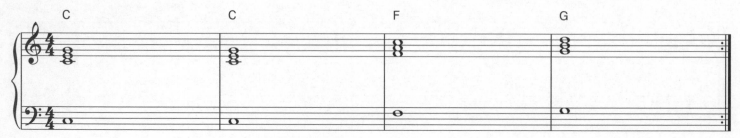

Example 7

♩ = 84 **Simple Rock**

Example 8

♩ = 84 **Pop**

Example 9

♩ = 80 **Pop**

Example 10

♩ = 100 **Simple Rock**

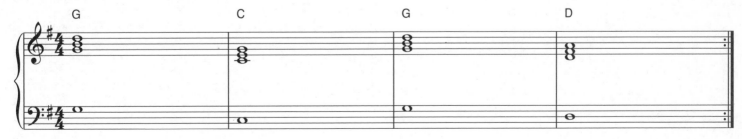

GRADE 1 PLAYBACK

Example 1

Example 2

Example 3

TOP TIP Notice that quavers (eighth notes) are featured in the playback test at Grade 1. Listen carefully to the backing track to help you play these in time with the beat.

Example 4

Example 5

Example 6

Example 7

TOP TIP Playback at Initial and Grade 1 is always in a five-finger hand position. This means that you can concentrate on the notes without having to think about shifting your hands.

Example 8

Example 9

Example 10

GRADE 1 IMPROVISING

Example 1

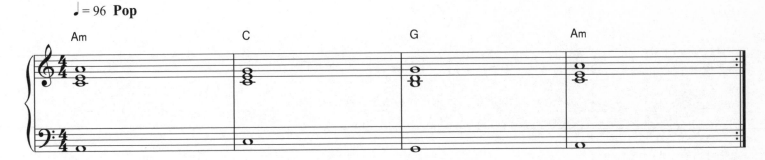

Example 2

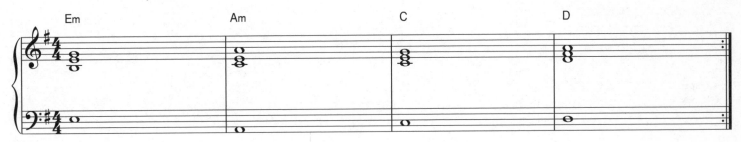

Example 3

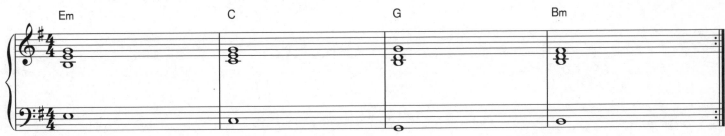

Example 4

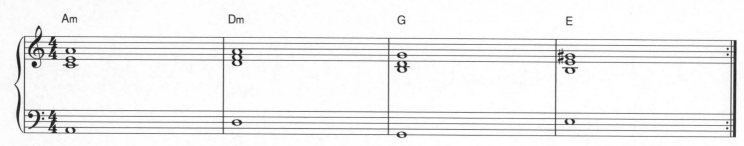

𝅘𝅥 = 76 **Ballad**

> **TOP TIP**
>
> The examples on this page are in very different styles: ballad and heavy rock. Consider what you could do in your improvising to bring out each style.

Example 5

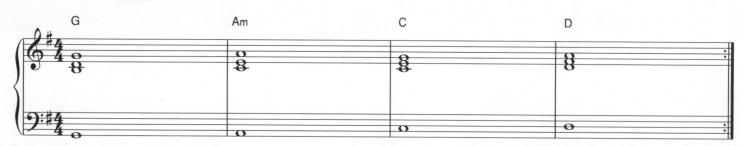

𝅘𝅥 = 72 **Ballad**

Example 6

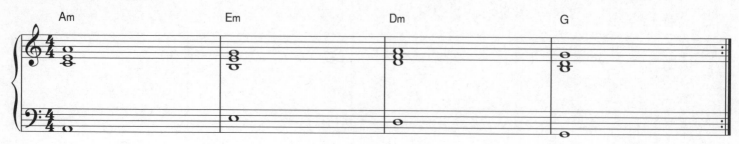

𝅘𝅥 = 90 **Heavy Rock**

Example 7

♩ = 100 **Heavy Rock**

Example 8

♩ = 96 **Pop**

Example 9

♩ = 96 **Heavy Rock**

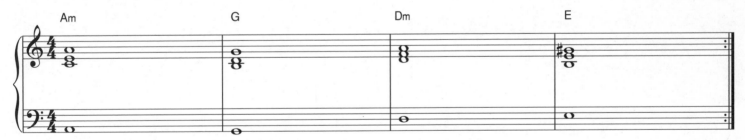

Example 10

♩ = 63 **Ballad**

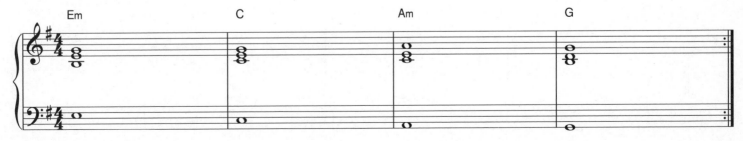

GRADE 2 PLAYBACK

Example 1

Example 2

Example 3

 TOP TIP Notice that ties are used in playback at Grade 2, creating a syncopated or off-beat effect. Listen carefully to the rhythms that feature ties to help you convey these when you perform them.

Example 4

Example 5

Example 6

Example 7

TOP TIP Accents are used in playback at Grade 2. Be sure to bring these out in your playing to add interest and variety to the music.

Example 8

Example 9

Example 10

GRADE 2 IMPROVISING

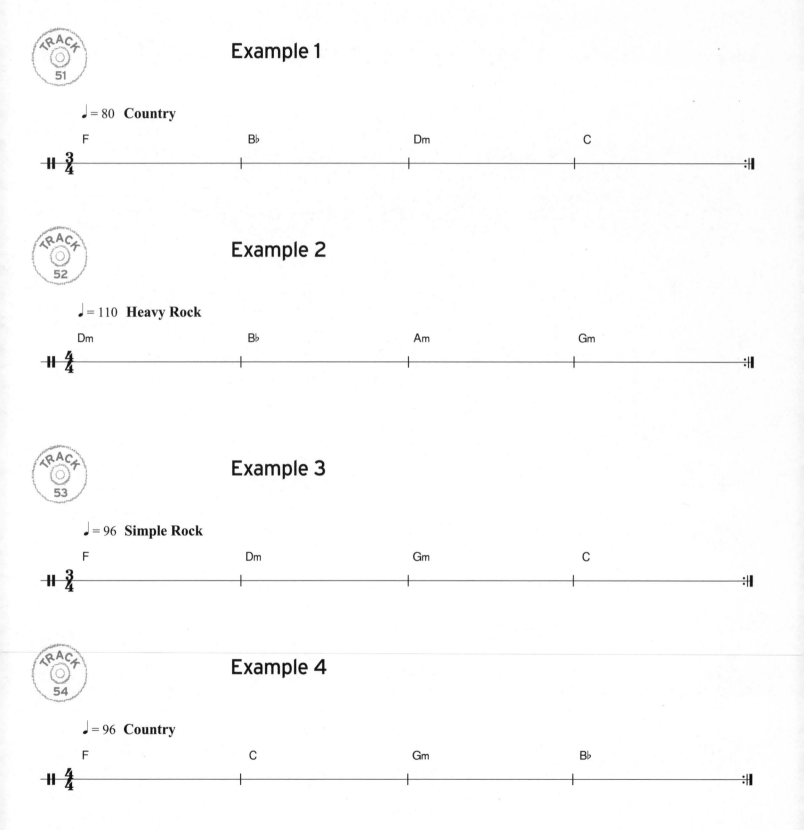

TRACK 51

Example 1

♩ = 80 **Country**

| F | B♭ | Dm | C |

𝄆 3/4 𝄇

TRACK 52

Example 2

♩ = 110 **Heavy Rock**

| Dm | B♭ | Am | Gm |

𝄆 4/4 𝄇

TRACK 53

Example 3

♩ = 96 **Simple Rock**

| F | Dm | Gm | C |

𝄆 3/4 𝄇

TRACK 54

Example 4

♩ = 96 **Country**

| F | C | Gm | B♭ |

𝄆 4/4 𝄇

Example 5

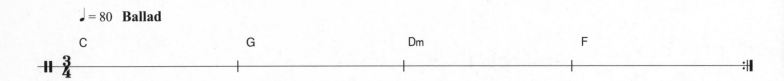

♩ = 80 **Ballad**

| C | G | Dm | F |

3/4

TOP TIP Notice that country style has been introduced at Grade 2. Listen to some country music and try to incorporate some of its stylistic features into your improvising.

Example 6

♩ = 120 **Heavy Rock**

| Dm | A | G | G |

4/4

Example 7

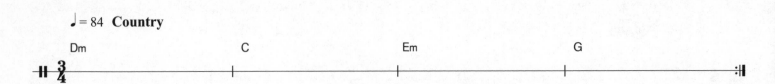

♩ = 84 **Country**

| Dm | C | Em | G |

3/4

Example 8

♩ = 70 **Ballad**

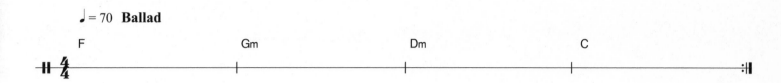

| F | Gm | Dm | C |

Example 9

♩ = 82 **Ballad**

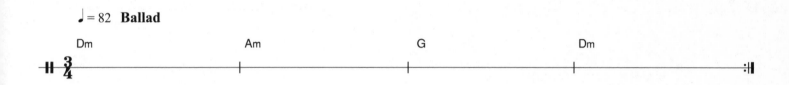

| Dm | Am | G | Dm |

TOP TIP Who are your improvising heroes? Listen to as much music as you can to gain inspiration from the greats of improvisation.

Example 10

♩ = 90 **Country**

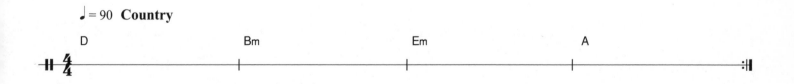

| D | Bm | Em | A |